Southern Appalachia

AMERICAN

REGIONAL COOKING
LIBRARY
Culture, Tradition,
and History

African American

American Indian

Amish and Mennonite

California

Hawaiian

Louisiana

Mexican American

Mid–Atlantic

Midwest

New England

Northwest

Southern Appalachia

Southern

Texas

Thanksgiving

Southern Appalachia

Mason Crest Publishers

Philadelphia

Mason Crest Publishers, Inc.
370 Reed Road
Broomall, Pennsylvania 19008
(866) MCP-BOOK (toll free)
www.masoncrest.com

First printing
1 2 3 4 5 6 7 8 9 10

ISBN 1-59084-620-6
ISBN 1-59084-609-5 (series)

Library of Congress Cataloging-in-Publication Data

Libal, Joyce.
   Southern Appalachian cooking / [compiled by Joyce Libal ; recipes by Patricia Therrien].
      p. cm. — (American regional cooking library)
   ISBN 1-59084-620-6
   1.   Cookery, American—Southern style—Juvenile literature. 2.   Cookery—Appalachian Region, Southern—Juvenile literature. I. Therrien, Patricia. II. Title. III. Series.
   TX715.2.S68L52 2005
   641.5975—dc22

                                    2004010071
Compiled by Joyce Libal.
Recipes by Patricia Therrien.
Recipes tested and prepared by Bonni Phelps.
Produced by Harding House Publishing Services, Inc., Vestal, New York.
Interior design by Dianne Hodack.
Cover design by Michelle Bouch.
Printed and bound in the Hashemite Kingdom of Jordan.

6583

Contents

Introduction
by the Culinary Institute of America

Cooking is a dynamic profession, one that presents some of the greatest challenges and offers some of the greatest rewards. Since 1946, the Culinary Institute of America has provided aspiring and seasoned foodservice professionals with the knowledge and skills needed to become leaders and innovators in this industry.

Here at the CIA, we teach our students the fundamental culinary techniques they need to build a sound foundation for their foodservice careers. There is always another level of perfection for them to achieve and another skill to master. Our rigorous curriculum provides them with a springboard to continued growth and success.

Food is far more than simply sustenance or the source of energy to fuel you and your family through life's daily regimen. It conjures memories throughout life, summoning up the smell, taste, and flavor of simpler times. Cooking is more than an art and a science; it provides family history. Food prepared with care epitomizes the love, devotion, and culinary delights that you offer to your friends and family.

A cuisine provides a way to express and establish customs—the way a food should taste and the flavors and aromas associated with that food. Cuisines are more than just a collection of ingredients, cooking utensils, and dishes from a geographic location; they are elements that are critical to establishing a culinary identity.

When you can accurately read a recipe, you can trace a variety of influences by observing which ingredients are selected and also by noting the technique that is used. If you research the historical origins of a recipe, you may find ingredients that traveled from East to West or from the New World to the Old. Traditional methods of cooking a dish may have changed with the times or to meet the special challenges.

The history of cooking illustrates the significance of innovation and the trading or sharing of ingredients and tools between societies. Although the various cooking vessels over the years have changed, the basic cooking methods have remained the same. Through adaptation, a recipe created years ago in a remote corner of the world could today be recognized by many throughout the globe.

When observing the customs of different societies, it becomes apparent that food brings people together. It is the common thread that we share and that we value. Regardless of the occasion, food is present to celebrate and to comfort. Through food we can experience other cultures and lands, learning the significance of particular ingredients and cooking techniques.

As you begin your journey through the culinary arts, keep in mind the power that food and cuisine holds. When passed from generation to generation, family heritage and traditions remain strong. Become familiar with the dishes your family has enjoyed through the years and play a role in keeping them alive. Don't be afraid to embellish recipes along the way – creativity is what cooking is all about.

Southern Appalachian Culture, History, and Traditions

People came to America from many countries, spreading out from the eastern coast. During the eighteenth century, settlers began to venture across the Appalachian Mountains, a rugged barrier to westward migration. Some people who crossed the mountains were attracted by the rugged beauty and fertile soil of the area, and they decided to stay. People from the Scottish lowlands, Northern Ireland, and Northern England all moved into the area. Like other immigrants, they were seeking both economic opportunity and religious freedom. In addition to farming, many people worked in mines, and immigrants from countries such as Poland and Hungary were recruited to do this work. People from Germany also moved to the area. Today, the people who live in the southern Appalachian Mountains speak a dialect that has developed from the merging of all these cultures. Some people refer to this as a hillbilly dialect, while others point out its similarity to the way Scottish and Irish people speak.

Appalachia is an Indian word that means "endless mountain range." Southern Appalachia includes parts of southwestern Pennsylvania, western Maryland, western Virginia, western South Carolina, western North Carolina, Kentucky, and Tennessee. The only state that lies entirely within this geographic area is West Virginia.

The mountain terrain served to isolate residents from outside influences. Of necessity, these were a self-sufficient people, hunting, growing, and making most of what they needed to survive. Extended families had close ties, and people helped their neighbors. Although formal education was usually limited, people became skilled craftsmen. Wood that was found in the area was used to make musical instruments such as dulcimers, fiddles, and mandolins, for which the area is still well known today.

Appalachia is famous for its music, created from a unique blend of Southern blues and Irish folk music. Songs became a way of keeping stories alive and passing them from one generation to another. Dancing, such as square dancing and clogging, is also an important part of the culture. African-Americans brought the banjo to the Appalachians, and they too had a strong influence on Appalachian music.

The plentiful woods that grew on the mountainsides were also used to build cabins and barns. Native plants and animals were also utilized. American Indians were already living in the area, and they taught newcomers about edible wild plants. Nothing went to waste on the farm.

Preserving food to last through the winter was an important part of Appalachian life. Vegetables and fruits were canned and dried. People made many types of pickles and preserved some vegetables, such as potatoes, by keeping them underground. Many families had a stone smokehouse where they smoked meat, and even today the area is famous for its cured hams.

Nowadays people in the Southern Appalachian area live in the same manner as in the rest of the country. New residents who hold professional positions such as lawyers and bankers have joined the descendants of the original settlers. Fancy restaurants serve all types of food, but in many homes, early food traditions still remain. People in other areas of the country are now becoming interested in Southern Appalachian cuisine. This book offers a selection of these traditional recipes.

Before you cook...

If you haven't done much cooking before, you may find recipe books a little confusing. Certain words and terms can seem unfamiliar. You may find the measurements difficult to understand. What appears to be an easy or familiar dish may contain ingredients you've never heard of before. You might not understand what utensil the recipe calls for you to use, or you might not be sure what the recipe is asking you to do.

Reading the pages in this section before you get started may help you understand the directions better so that your cooking goes more smoothly. You can also refer back to these pages whenever you run into questions.

Safety Tips

Cooking involves handling very hot and very sharp objects, so being careful is common sense. What's more, you want to be certain that anything you plan on putting in your mouth is safe to eat. If you follow these easy tips, you should find that cooking can be both fun and safe.

Before you cook...

- Always wash your hands before and after handling food. This is particularly important after you handle raw meats, poultry, and eggs, as bacteria called salmonella can live on these uncooked foods. You can't see or smell salmonella, but these germs can make you or anyone who swallows them very sick.
- Make a habit of using potholders or oven mitts whenever you handle pots and pans from the oven or microwave.
- Always set pots, pans, and knives with their handles away from counter edges. This way you won't risk catching your sleeves on them—and any younger children in the house won't be in danger of grabbing something hot or sharp.
- Don't leave perishable food sitting out of the refrigerator for more than an hour or two.
- Wash all raw fruits and vegetables to remove dirt and chemicals.
- Use a cutting board when chopping vegetables or fruit, and always cut away from yourself.
- Don't overheat grease or oil—but if grease or oil does catch fire, don't try to extinguish the flames with water. Instead, throw baking soda or salt on the fire to put it out. Turn all stove burners off.
- If you burn yourself, immediately put the burn under cold water, as this will prevent the burn from becoming more painful.
- Never put metal dishes or utensils in the microwave. Use only microwave-proof dishes.
- Wash cutting boards and knives thoroughly after cutting meat, fish or poultry — especially when raw and before using the same tools to prepare other foods such as vegetables and cheese. This will prevent the spread of bacteria such as salmonella.
- Keep your hands away from any moving parts of appliances, such as mixers.
- Unplug any appliance, such as a mixer, blender, or food processor before assembling for use or disassembling after use.

Metric Conversion Table

Most cooks in the United States use measuring containers based on an eight-ounce cup, a teaspoon, and a tablespoon. Meanwhile, cooks in Canada and Europe are more apt to use metric measurements. The recipes in this book use cups, teaspoons, and tablespoons—but you can convert these measurements to metric by using the table below.

Temperature
To convert Fahrenheit degrees to Celsius, subtract 32 and multiply by .56.

212°F = 100°C
(this is the boiling point of water)
250°F = 110°C
275°F = 135°C
300°F = 150°C
325°F = 160°C
350°F = 180°C
375°F = 190°C
400°F = 200°C

Liquid Measurements
1 teaspoon = 5 milliliters
1 tablespoon = 15 milliliters
1 fluid ounce = 30 milliliters
1 cup = 240 milliliters
1 pint = 480 milliliters
1 quart = 0.95 liters
1 gallon = 3.8 liters

Measurements of Mass or Weight
1 ounce = 28 grams
8 ounces = 227 grams
1 pound (16 ounces) = 0.45 kilograms
2.2 pounds = 1 kilogram

Measurements of Length
¼ inch = 0.6 centimeters
½ inch = 1.25 centimeters
1 inch = 2.5 centimeters

Pan Sizes

Baking pans are usually made in standard sizes. The pans used in the United States are roughly equivalent to the following metric pans:

9-inch cake pan = 23-centimeter pan
11x7-inch baking pan = 28x18-centimeter baking pan
13x9-inch baking pan = 32.5x23-centimeter baking pan
9x5-inch loaf pan = 23x13-centimeter loaf pan
2-quart casserole = 2-liter casserole

Useful Tools, Utensils, Dishes

cast iron skillet electric mixer pancake griddle

pastry blender rubber spatula whisk

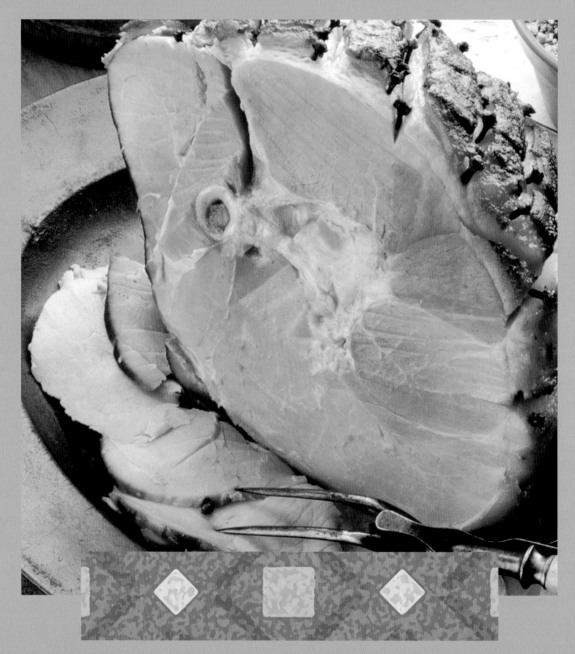

Cooking Glossary

cream A term used to describe mixing sugar with butter or shortening until they are light and well blended.

cut Mix solid shortening or butter into flour, usually by using a pastry blender or two knives and making short, chopping strokes until the mixture looks like small pellets.

dredge Drag or toss meat lightly into a seasoning mixture; be sure to cover the entire piece of meat.

fillets Thin strips of boneless fish or meat.

mince Cut into very small pieces.

set When a food preparation has completed the thickening process and can be sliced.

simmer Gently boiling, so that the surface of the liquid just ripples gently.

whisk Stir briskly with a wire whisk.

Special Southern Appalachian Flavors

grits

ham

nuts

peanuts

sorghum

Southern Appalachian Recipes

Baked Grits and Cheese

Eating grits for breakfast is a Southern tradition.

Preheat oven to 450° Fahrenheit.

Ingredients:

4 tablespoons butter
1 tablespoon **minced** *onion*
1 tablespoon minced garlic
2 cups water
2 cups milk
1 teaspoon salt
1 cup yellow stone–ground grits (not instant)
½ cup cream cheese (softened to room temperature)
1¼ cups grated cheddar cheese
pepper
3 tablespoons chopped fresh chives

Cooking utensils you'll need:
measuring cups
measuring spoons
large saucepan
wooden spoon
whisk
small baking dish

Directions:

Melt 3 tablespoons of butter in the saucepan, add onion and garlic, and cook until onion is translucent. Stir in water, milk, and salt, and bring mixture to a boil, stirring occasionally. Immediately reduce heat so mixture just *simmers*. *Whisk* mixture constantly while slowly pouring in the grits. Simmer and thicken for 15 minutes, stirring constantly with the wooden spoon to break up any lumps. Remove from heat, and stir in cream cheese, ¾ cup cheddar cheese, 2 tablespoons chives, and a couple shakes of pepper. Grease the baking dish with the remaining tablespoon of butter, pour the grits into the dish, and top with remaining cheese. Bake for 10 minutes, and sprinkle with remaining chives before serving.

Appalachian Food History

The word "grits" may come from Old English *grytt* (meaning bran) or *greot* (meaning ground). Although grits are made from corn, they are most often served for breakfast rather than used as a vegetable. Grits come from hominy, which is made from corn kernels that have been soaked in an alkaline solution. Hominy is dried and coarsely ground to make grits. American Indians were probably the first ones to make hominy and grits. Today, many commercial producers of grits use regular dried corn kernels rather than hominy. As you'll discover when you cook this food, grits become quite thick when mixed with hot liquids. Many people enjoy eating this like porridge for breakfast. Some people sweeten it with sugar.

Country Ham and Red-Eye Gravy

Here's another Appalachian breakfast favorite.

Ingredients:

1 thin slice of cooked ham
½ cup strong black coffee
6 tablespoons cola
2 tablespoons butter

Cooking utensils you'll need:
measuring cup
measuring spoon
cast iron skillet

Directions:

Place the ham in the cast iron skillet, cook each side until it is lightly browned (about 1 minute) over medium heat, and remove the ham from the pan. Add coffee and cola to the pan, increase heat to high, and scrape the ham pieces from the bottom of the pan as you boil the liquid for about 30 seconds. Stir in the butter, and continue *simmering* for another 30 seconds. Serve hot gravy over the ham.

Tips:

Many people make red-eye gravy without the cola.

Grits and biscuits are a traditional accompaniment to this dish. The biscuits are used to "sop up" the extra gravy.

Appalachian Food History

True country hams might look a bit dehydrated to you. That's because they are salt cured rather than sugar cured. Many of those hams have had water added to them and are ready to be popped in the oven. Country ham, on the other hand, should be covered with water and soaked overnight in the refrigerator. This water should then be discarded and new water poured over the ham. The ham is then boiled for a few hours before being removed from the water and placed in the oven.

Red-eye gravy was first made with country ham. Some people think the name comes from the fact that the crispy pieces of ham left in the skillet create a small amount of reddish fat that rises to the surface of the gravy in a round shape. A legend, however, attributes the name to General Andrew Jackson, who became the seventh president of the United States. According to this story, General Jackson's cook had been drinking whiskey, and the next day his eyes were very red. General Jackson was hungry and asked the cook to make some ham and gravy that were as red as the cook's eyes. Still another possibility for the name lies in the gravy's ingredients—the coffee and cola, with enough caffeine to "get the red out" of tired eyes.

Appalachian Food History and Traditions

The sorghum cane plant originated in Africa and was first grown in the southern part of the United States by African Americans. (African Americans are also credited with introducing several other plants to Southern Appalachia, including okra, black-eyed peas, and watermelons.) The sweet syrup that is derived from sorghum became a staple food in rural areas of the South and Southern Appalachian states, where it was used as a substitute for sugar when baking, as well as for syrup on pancakes. Farm families grew their own cane and took it to local mills for processing. Mill owners usually received a portion of the syrup in exchange for processing the cane. Today, sorghum syrup, which was plentiful and inexpensive in the past, can be more expensive than other syrups. Since it is thick and has a strong flavor, however, you may find that you don't need to use as much.

Many traditions and beliefs once governed the daily lives of the Appalachian mountain folk. Many of these had to do with food and meal times. For instance, don't talk about your nightmares before you eat your pancakes: if you tell a bad dream before breakfast it will come true. And don't act too happy while you're waiting for those pancakes either: if you whistle before breakfast, you will cry before dusk.

Sorghum plants

Buttermilk Pancakes with Sorghum Syrup

For a change of pace, eat your pancakes with the sweet-tasting traditional syrup of Southern Appalachia.

Ingredients:

1 cup self-rising flour
¼ cup melted butter
2 eggs
⅓ cup buttermilk
cold butter
sorghum syrup

Cooking utensils you'll need:
measuring cups
mixing bowl
pancake griddle

Directions:

Put the flour in the mixing bowl, and stir in butter and eggs. Add the buttermilk slowly as you continue stirring until no lumps remain. Use the ¼ measuring cup to pour batter onto the hot griddle. When outside edges of the pancakes begin to dry and the center is bubbly, check the bottom. When it's as brown as desired, flip the pancake over to cook the second side. Serve with cold pats of butter and warmed sorghum syrup.

Tips:

It is important to use self-rising flour in this recipe because baking soda is not among the ingredients. If you only have all-purpose flour in your home, add ½ teaspoon baking soda to the recipe.

To determine if the pancake griddle is hot enough, toss a couple drops of water onto it. If they sizzle and immediately evaporate, it's time to start cooking the pancakes.

Honey Facts

Honey is humanity's oldest sweetener. In fact, ancient cave paintings exist that depict people gathering honey. Beekeeping is a traditional skill of rural Southern Appalachia, but honeybees are not native to North America. Europeans introduced "white man's flies," as American Indians called them, to the Americas.

In order to produce a single pound of honey, bees gather nectar from as many as 2 million flowers and fly as many as 40,000 miles!

Smoky Mountain Muffins

Preheat oven to 400° Fahrenheit.

Ingredients:

2 cups flour
4 teaspoons baking powder
½ teaspoon salt
1 egg
4 tablespoons cooking oil
2 tablespoons honey
¼ cup milk

Cooking utensils you'll need:
measuring cups
measuring spoons
2 mixing bowls
whisk
muffin pan

Directions:

Grease the muffin pan, and set it aside. Stir together flour, baking powder, and salt, and set aside. Whisk egg with oil, honey, and milk. Pour dry ingredients into wet ingredients, and stir just until combined. Divide batter equally between muffin cups, and bake for 25 minutes (or until golden brown).

Tips:

Never over beat muffin batter.

When measuring honey, molasses, or other sticky ingredients, measure oil, water, or milk in the measuring cup first. That way the measuring cup will be coated and the sticky ingredient will slide out easier.

Add a tasty surprise to each muffin by putting just 2 tablespoons of batter in each muffin cup, then add 1 teaspoon of fruit preserves to each cup, and top them off with the remaining batter before baking.

You can also add fresh fruit to these muffins.

Skillet Corn Bread

Preheat oven to 450° Fahrenheit.

Ingredients:

2 teaspoons bacon drippings
1¾ cups cornmeal
1 teaspoon baking powder
1 teaspoon baking soda
1 teaspoon salt
1 egg
2 cups buttermilk

Cooking utensils you'll need:
measuring cups
measuring spoons
2 mixing bowls
cast iron skillet

Directions:

Grease the cast iron skillet with bacon drippings. Stir together dry ingredients in one bowl. Mix egg and buttermilk in second bowl. Pour dry ingredients into wet ingredients, and stir until combined. Pour into skillet, and bake for 15 minutes (until lightly browned).

Tips:

Unless instructed to do otherwise in recipes, always use large eggs when baking.

In the old days, women routinely saved bacon grease for cooking purposes. If you don't have bacon grease, you can grease the pan with shortening.

Warm cornbread tastes great with butter and a little molasses or sorghum syrup.

Appalachian Food History

American Indians were cultivating corn long before Spanish explorers first arrived on American shores. The plant originated in Mexico as many as 4,000 years ago. Corn was of immense importance to Native people, and many ceremonies developed concerning its cultivation and use. Early European settlers quickly adopted corn into their own diets and began to grow it as a staple crop. Today, it is the third largest crop grown in the world, exceeded only by wheat and rice.

Appalachian Food History

Kentucky Hot Brown was first served in the early 1920s at the Brown Hotel in Louisville, Kentucky. Today, there are several variations of this dish that was first made by Fred Schmidt while working on the night shift. According to the story, Mr. Schmidt invented the open-faced sandwich when he became bored with other foods that he was serving to the hotel's up-scale late-night crowd.

Kentucky Hot Brown

Cooking utensils you'll need:
measuring cups
measuring spoons
saucepan
toaster
small baking dish

Preheat oven to 400° Fahrenheit.

Ingredients:

Hot Brown:
1½ cups cheese sauce
1 slice bread
1 slice cooked country ham
1 slice cooked turkey
¼ cup shredded sharp cheddar cheese
¼ cup shredded Parmesan cheese
paprika to taste
2 slices cooked bacon
tomato or fresh peach slices

Cheese Sauce:
2 tablespoons butter
2 tablespoons flour
¼ teaspoon salt
white pepper to taste
1 cup milk
1 cup shredded mild or medium cheddar cheese

Directions:

Melt the butter in the saucepan. Stir in flour, salt, and pepper, and cook for about a minute, stirring constantly. Slowly stir in milk, and continue to cook and stir over medium heat until thickened. Stir in 1 cup mild or medium cheddar cheese, and heat until melted. Toast the bread. Put 2 tablespoons of cheese sauce into the baking dish, place the toast on top of the cheese sauce, and pour 3 more tablespoons of cheese sauce on top of the toast, followed by the ham. Put 2 tablespoons of Parmesan cheese on top of the ham, followed by the turkey. Layer on 3 tablespoons of cheese sauce, followed by the sharp cheese and remaining Parmesan cheese. Add a couple shakes of paprika, top with bacon, and bake for about 15 minutes (until heated through). Serve with tomato or peach slices.

Iced Tea Syrup

Store this syrup in your refrigerator, and use it anytime you want to stir up a glass of iced tea instantly.

Ingredients:

14 tea bags (or 1 cup loose tea)
3½ cups water
2½ cups sugar

Directions:

Bring the water to a boil over high heat. Remove from heat, place tea bags or loose tea in kettle, cover, and allow tea to steep for about 5 minutes. Remove tea bags or strain tea and stir in the sugar. Store tea syrup in a glass jar with a tight-fitting lid in the refrigerator. Whenever you want a glass of iced tea, just place ¼ cup of tea syrup in a glass, and add cold water and ice.

Cooking utensils you'll need:
measuring cups
tea kettle
strainer (if using loose tea)

Southern Appalachian Traditions

Girls were taught to be obedient, quiet, and devoted to others, while boys learned to be proud, independent, and aggressive. The wife in a family was subservient to her husband, sometimes walking behind him when in public. When guests arrived for dinner, women served the men and then ate separately from them. Women weren't usually seen in public, and when going to church they often wore a veil over their eyes or entire face. Women and men were not to look into each other's eyes unless they were married. Most marriages were arranged by parents for their children and took place when children were at a relatively young age (usually between fifteen and eighteen for girls and between eighteen and twenty for boys).

Most girls became pregnant within the first year of marriage and almost every year thereafter. Not surprisingly, many women died at a young age because of numerous pregnancies and lack of adequate medical care. When someone died, a bell was rung to announce the death to other people in the territory. Because the bell was rung once for each year of the person's life, many people could tell who died by the number of times the bell tolled.

Modern education and the spread of television have changed life in Appalachia. The old traditions and customs linger, however, in some of the old families.

Appalachian Hotdog Sauce

People in different areas of the country like to top their hotdogs in different ways. Here's a meat sauce that is typical of Appalachian hotdogs.

Ingredients:

1 pound lean ground beef
1 large onion, **minced**
2½ tablespoons chili powder
¼ teaspoon garlic powder
water

Cooking utensils you'll need:
measuring spoons
skillet with lid

Directions:

Place beef and onion in skillet over medium heat, and cook until meat is well browned and onion is translucent. Stir in seasonings, add water just to cover ingredients, cover skillet, lower heat, and *simmer* for 1 hour. Serve warm on hot dogs.

Appalachian Food History

Hunting was a way of life in the Appalachian Mountains and is still popular today. Along with deer and rabbits, squirrel was often hunted and served as a popular breakfast food. While city squirrels are used to people and may frequent the bird feeder in your yard, country squirrels are more wary. A hunter had to settle down in the woods and sit very still, sometimes for long periods of time, until a squirrel came within shooting range. Squirrel is often dredged in flour, fried, and served with gravy. Its flavor is similar to chicken.

The Appalachian Mountains are filled with superstition—and some of them dictate the proper way to hunt. For instance, if you wrap a black horsehair around your wrist, it will make you shoot straight. But if you are out hunting and see your shadow, you might as well go home, as you'll not get any game that day.

Baked Beans

Make protein-rich beans as a side dish or main dish.

Preheat oven to 400° Fahrenheit.

Ingredients:

*½ pound lean ground beef
one 31-ounce can pork and beans
1 medium onion, chopped
½ green pepper, chopped
½ cup ketchup
½ cup brown sugar packed
2 tablespoons mustard
4 slices bacon*

*Cooking utensils you'll need:
measuring cup
measuring spoon
skillet
9x13-inch baking dish*

Directions:

Place meat in skillet over medium heat, and cook until browned. Stir in remaining ingredients except bacon. Pour into baking dish, place bacon slices on top, and bake for 40 minutes.

Appalachian Food History

When growing beans or other vegetables, Appalachian farmers used a calendar or almanac that delineated the days of the month by signs based on the stars and the moon. Farmers picked the series of days with the most favorable signs for planting or harvesting their crops. The best time to plant crops with fruits above ground was while the moon was waxing (growing bigger), and they planted crops with "fruits" below ground (like potatoes, radishes, peanuts) while the moon was waning (growing smaller). Here are the signs of the Zodiac and a few tips that apply to food production:

Aries (March 21 - April 20)
Good for cultivating the ground, planting beets and onions, and hunting. Bad for planting and transplanting other crops.

Taurus (April 21 - May 21)
Good for all root crops and above-ground crops, and also for hunting and fishing.

Gemini (May 22 - June 21)
Good for planting all crops, also for preserving jellies and pickles.

Cancer (June 22 - July 22)
Best for planting above-ground and root crops. Good for cooking and fishing.

Leo (July 23 - August 21)
Bad for planting or transplanting.

Virgo (August 22 - September 23)
Bad for planting.

Libra (September 24 - October 23)
Good for planting above-ground crops and flowering plants.

Scorpio (October 24 - November 22)
Best for flowers and above-ground crops. Good for all other crops, fishing, and hunting.

Sagittarius (November 23 - December 22)
Good for baking and preserving. Bad for transplanting.

Capricorn (December 23 - January 20)
Best for root crops. Good for flowers and above-ground crops.

Aquarius (January 21 - February 19)
Good for above-ground crops.

Pisces (February 20 - March 20)
Good for planting and transplanting above-ground crops.

Appalachian Food History

Tomatoes originated in South America thousands of years ago. Like the potato, which is also from South America, it is a member of the nightshade family. People from many cultures now include fried ripe tomatoes in their cuisine, but fried green tomatoes are an original Southern dish.

Fried Green Tomatoes

A homemaker who had a bumper crop of tomatoes and needed to find new ways to use them probably developed this now-traditional dish.

Ingredients:

½ cup cornmeal
½ cup flour
salt and pepper
1 egg
1 cup milk
3 or 4 green tomatoes, cored and sliced
cooking oil

Cooking utensils you'll need:
measuring cup
mixing bowl
plate
skillet

Directions:

Mix cornmeal and flour on the plate and add a couple shakes of salt and pepper. Put 2 or 3 tablespoons of cooking oil in the skillet over medium heat. Stir the egg and milk together in the bowl. Dip tomato slices in the egg mixture, dredge in cornmeal mixture, and fry turning once to brown both sides. Serve this side dish hot.

Tip:

A cast iron skillet is perfect for cooking foods like the cornbread in the previous recipe. However, don't use one when cooking high-acid foods, like tomatoes or pineapples. Iron can leach out of the pan into these types of food, imparting a very unpleasant taste.

Country Round Steak

Preheat oven to 250° Fahrenheit.

Ingredients:

1 pound round steak
1 tablespoon canola oil
½ cup flour
½ teaspoon salt
¼ teaspoon pepper
¼ cup water

Cooking utensils you'll need:
measuring cup
measuring spoons
mixing bowl
skillet
13x9-inch baking dish
aluminum foil

Directions:

Wash the meat, pat it dry with paper towels, and cut into 4 equal-sized pieces. Put oil in the skillet, and place it over medium heat. Mix the flour, salt, and pepper, and *dredge* the meat pieces in it. Fry the meat until browned on both sides, place browned meat in the baking dish, pour water into the dish, cover with foil, and bake for 1½ hours.

Appalachian Food History

Round steak became a favorite because it is less expensive than most other types of steak. It is a lean cut of meat that can be rather tough if not prepared correctly. Historically, the Appalachian Mountains have been economically depressed. This is partially due to the rugged environment, which has not been conducive to the types of development that bring high-paying jobs. Mining and farming were the major employers. Now more economic opportunity exists for individuals and families to lift themselves out of the legacy of poverty that has been associated with the area.

Fried Catfish

Ingredients:

4 catfish fillets
cooking oil
¾ cup cornmeal
¼ cup flour
2 teaspoons salt
¼ teaspoon garlic powder (optional)
1 teaspoon cayenne pepper (optional)

Cooking utensils you'll need:
measuring cups
measuring spoons
heavy-duty plastic bag
cooking thermometer
deep-sided pan for frying
long-handled slotted spoon

Directions:

Wash fish, and pat them dry with paper towels. Pour 2 or 3 inches of cooking oil into the pan (enough to cover the fish), attach the thermometer to the pan, and bring the oil to 350° Fahrenheit over medium heat. Put the dry ingredients in the plastic bag, and shake to mix. Put catfish in the bag, shake to coat, put a fish on the long-handled spoon, and carefully place it in the oil. Repeat with remaining fish, and fry until browned (usually 5 or 6 minutes). Place fish on paper towels to drain off some of the fat before serving.

Appalachian Food Tradition

According to the mountainfolk, fish bite best at night. And if you play a fiddle, the fish will come to the surface of the water. (Fish love music!) Don't play your harmonica while you fish, though, or you'll call all the snakes for miles around.

Kentucky Burgoo

Cooking utensils you'll need:
measuring cup
measuring spoons
stockpot

Ingredients:

2 pounds chicken parts
1 pound beef stew meat (If using
  beef on bones, add another pound.)
2 tablespoons cooking oil
4 cups water
½ teaspoon black pepper
½ teaspoon cayenne pepper
1½ teaspoons salt
1 small can tomato paste
1 garlic clove, **minced**
1 bay leaf

5 or 6 potatoes, peeled and **diced**
1 onion, chopped
1 head cabbage, chopped
3 or 4 tomatoes, peeled and chopped
(see "Tips")
2 carrots, sliced
1 green bell pepper, chopped
4 tablespoons Worcestershire sauce
1 cup butter beans
1 cup sliced okra
3 ears of corn (see "Tips")

Directions:

Heat oil in the stockpot, and brown the beef. Add chicken, water, black pepper, cayenne pepper, and salt. Cover pot, cook 40 minutes (until meat is very tender), remove from heat. When meat is cool enough to handle, remove the bones and chicken skin, cut meat into bite sized pieces, and return to pot. Add remaining ingredients except okra and corn, cover and *simmer* for 2 hours, stirring occasionally and adding more water as necessary to keep the ingredients from sticking to the bottom of the pot. Add okra and corn, and cook 15 minutes. Add more salt and pepper if necessary, remove bay leaf, and serve.

Tips:

To easily peel tomatoes, first rub them firmly all over with the dull edge of a butter knife.

To cut corn off the cob, hold it upright and steady with the stem side down. With a sharp knife in your other hand, slice downward, cutting off a few rows of corn kernels. Then go back and gently scrape that area of the cob to get more of the corn juice. Some people like to place the cob in the center tube of an angel-food cake pan so the cut kernels fall into the pan. You still need to hold the cob steady as you cut when using this method. If fresh corn is not available, use frozen corn.

Appalachian Food History

During the mid-1700s, the word "burgoo" was used to refer to oatmeal porridge or a meal of hardtack (bread made from just flour and water) and molasses. Modern burgoo is infinitely more appealing.

The original burgoo was served aboard ships. It was converted into a meat-based stew in the United States. There are many different recipes for burgoo. Basically, burgoo can contain whatever ingredients are available to the cook. Veal, lamb, even squirrels can be used along with whatever vegetables are ripe or in storage.

Appalachian Food History

In the mountains of North Carolina, "pulled-pork" or "picked-pork" barbecue usually means a whole 100- to 150-pound pig, roasted over a fire, for as many as twelve hours. The meat becomes so tender that it is easily pulled or picked off the bone, hence the name. The wood used for pork barbecue usually comes from a tree that bears either fruit or nuts. Hickory and oak are commonly used, but nowadays, propane may also be used to fuel the grill.

Pork barbecue has been cooked in North Carolina since the eighteenth century. Traditionally, men roast the pig while women make side dishes such as cabbage slaw, corn bread or hush puppies, baked beans, and boiled potatoes. In Eastern North Carolina, a vinegar-based barbecue sauce may be put on the meat before eating. In Western North Carolina, however, the sauce will usually have ketchup added to it, while in South Carolina it will probably include mustard. This traditional food is often served at fund-raising events.

The exact origin of pork barbecue is not clear, but it may have descended from Scottish/Irish boar roasts. American Indians also used fires to roast meat. Today, North Carolina is the number-two state for pork production in the nation.

North Carolina Barbecue

In North Carolina, barbecue means pork cooked slowly over a wood fire. Sauce may be added at the end, and the type of sauce used varies depending upon what part of the state it is made in. The inclusion of ketchup in the sauce below means it's from Western North Carolina.

Preheat oven to 325° Fahrenheit.

Ingredients:

6 or 7 pound pork shoulder
1 cup cider vinegar
1 cup water
½ cup ketchup
1 teaspoon chili powder
¼ teaspoon garlic powder
1 teaspoon pepper
2 teaspoons brown sugar, packed
1 tablespoon lemon juice
½ teaspoon salt

Cooking utensils you'll need:
roasting pan with cover or
baking pan and aluminum foil
measuring cups
measuring spoons
saucepan

Directions:

Wash meat, pat it dry with paper towels, place it pan, cover, and bake 1 hour for each pound of meat. Put remaining ingredients in saucepan, simmer for 1 minute, and allow to stand for at least 30 minutes before using. Allow meat to cool enough to handle, then remove skin, fat, and bone. If desired, place the pan of meat over a charcoal fire for about 30 minutes to develop a smoky flavor. Pour barbecue sauce over meat, and continue barbecuing for 15 more minutes. If you are not placing the meat on a barbecue grill, return it to the oven for at least 15 minutes before serving.

Tennessee Walnut Cookies

Chilling this dough overnight helps the walnut flavor permeate the dough and gives the finished cookies a super-nutty taste.

Ingredients:

1 cup brown sugar, packed
1 cup butter
1 egg
1 teaspoon vanilla
1 teaspoon black walnut flavoring
3 cups flour
¼ teaspoon salt
¼ teaspoon nutmeg
½ cup chopped black walnuts (or substitute English walnuts)

Cooking utensils you'll need:
measuring cups
measuring spoons
2 mixing bowls
plastic wrap
cookie sheet

Directions:

Cream sugar with butter, stir in egg, mix well, add vanilla and black walnut flavoring, and mix again. In a second bowl, mix flour, salt, and nutmeg. Pour the dry ingredients into the wet ingredients, and mix well. Stir in the walnuts, use your hands to shape the dough into logs that are about 1½ inches in diameter, wrap them in plastic wrap, and refrigerate until the next day. When you are ready to bake the cookies, preheat oven to 410° Fahrenheit, lightly grease the cookie sheet, thinly slice the logs, and bake cookies for 10 minutes (or until done).

Appalachian Food History

American Indians were eating black walnuts and using the sap of the tree for food at least 2,000 years before Europeans reached the Southern Appalachian states. This impressive tree is native to North America, and was used by colonists for medicinal purposes as well as for food, furniture, and to make gun stocks.

Overharvesting has increased the value of the larger trees that remain. Now the wood is used mostly as a veneer over less expensive woods when making furniture. In 1985, one large log from a black walnut tree that was hundreds of years old sold for $90,000!

For the past fifty years, Spencer, West Virginia has been holding the annual West Virginia Black Walnut Festival. The Little Kanawha Regional Council first got the idea to hold the festival back in 1954 when a man named Henry Young sold 2 million pounds of black walnuts. The council then realized black walnuts were a potential cash crop that could be sold by local farmers, and the next year they began to promote sales through the festival.

People who are lucky enough to have black walnut trees growing on their property realize how difficult it is to get to the edible nuts inside of the hard and sticky outer shells. In fact, people sometimes drive cars and pickup trucks over them to remove the outer shell. Even then, rubber gloves are necessary when handling the nuts, as they are covered with a black oily substance that stains both clothing and skin. The strong flavor of black walnuts is mellowed and improved by cooking.

Fried Apple Pies

Use dried fruit to make delicious individual pastries.

Ingredients:

3 cups dried apples
water
½ to ¾ cup brown sugar, packed
1 teaspoon cinnamon
2 cups flour
1 teaspoon baking powder
½ cup butter, softened to room temperature
cold milk or water
cooking oil
confectioners' sugar (powdered sugar)

Cooking utensils you'll need:
measuring cups
measuring spoons
saucepan
mixing bowl
pastry blender (optional)
rolling pin
fork
skillet

Directions:

Place apples in saucepan, add water to just cover them, place over medium heat, and *simmer* for 30 minutes. When apples begin to soften, add sugar, lower heat, and continue to cook for another 30 minutes. Mash the apples, stir in cinnamon, and set aside. Mix flour with baking powder, and cut in butter. Cut in milk or water 1 tablespoon at a time until dough is moist but still firm, and divide into 10 equal-sized pieces. Sprinkle extra flour on a flat surface, and roll one of the pieces to a 6-inch circle. Place 1 or 2 spoonfuls of apple filling on one side of the circle, moisten the edge of the circle with water if necessary, and fold the dough over to cover the filling. Use a fork to pinch the edges of the half circle closed, dipping the fork in flour if necessary. Repeat with remaining ingredients. Heat oil in skillet, fry pies until golden brown on both sides, and drain on paper towels. Sprinkle with powdered sugar, and serve warm.

Tips:

You can also make these pastries with other dried fruits such as peaches or apricots.

Nowadays, you can purchase dried apples at the grocery store or dry them yourself using an electric dehydrator. You can even use your oven by heating it to 120° Fahrenheit, placing ¼-inch apple slices on screens or baking racks on cookie sheets, popping them into the oven, and then turning the heat off. Turn the oven back up each time it cools down until the apples are dry.

Appalachian Food History

Apples are not native to North America but were one of the first fruits established by colonists. Many varieties of fresh apples last for many months in cool storage, but drying is one way to make them last even longer. In the past, apples were often dried on screens or cloths placed in the sun. The cloth or screen would be attached to a wooden frame and suspended between chairs. Someone had to watch over the apples as they dried to shoo birds and insects away from them. As the apples lose moisture, they darken and become leathery. The sugar and tartness are concentrated in these chewy treats.

Peanut Butter Pie

Ingredients:

prepared piecrust
1 cup flour
½ cup sugar
1 teaspoon salt
2 cups milk
3 egg yolks
2 tablespoons butter

1 tablespoon vanilla
1 cup peanut butter
½ cup confectioners' sugar (powdered sugar)
4 egg whites
¼ teaspoon cream of tartar
6 tablespoons sugar
½ teaspoon vanilla

Directions:

Bake crust according to package directions, and cool. Mix flour, sugar, and salt in saucepan. Stir in milk and 3 egg yolks, place over medium heat, bring to boil stirring constantly, *simmer* until thickened. Remove from heat, add butter and vanilla, stir until butter is melted, cool. Mix peanut butter with confectioners' sugar (mixture will be crumbly). Place half of crumb mixture in piecrust, and pour cooled filling on the crumbs. Beat egg whites with cream of tartar until soft peaks form. Gradually beat in the 6 tablespoons sugar and vanilla. Spread meringue on pie, top with remaining crumb mixture, and place under the broiler just until lightly browned. (Watch this closely as it does not take very long to brown and can burn very quickly.)

Tip:

If you want to try making your own piecrust, mix ¾ cup flour with ¼ teaspoon salt. *Cut* in 2 tablespoons shortening. When the mixture looks like meal, cut in another 2 tablespoons shortening. Cut in 1½ tablespoons cold water.

Gather the dough into a ball. Sprinkle flour on a flat surface such as a wooden cutting board and on a rolling pin. Place the dough on the flat surface and pat it a little to begin flattening it out. Lift it up and put a little flour under it. Begin rolling from the center outward and in all directions. Add more flour to the rolling pin as necessary. Lift up the edges of the dough and add more flour if necessary. When the dough is the size needed for the pie plate, fold it in half. Place the pie plate next to the dough, slide the dough into it, and open the folded dough up. Gently pat the dough into the pie plate, crimp the edges of the dough, and trim off any excess with a butter knife.

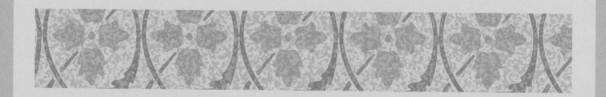

Appalachian Food History

Peanuts are another of the important foods that developed in South America. From there, they went to Africa before being brought to North America aboard slave ships. This high-protein food is not really a nut at all. Like beans, it is a legume. About half of the peanuts grown in the United States each year are processed to make peanut butter. Peanuts need a long, warm growing season and thrive in the Southern states. There was a time when most Southern farmers tended a peanut patch, growing enough peanuts for family use.

Kentucky Rebel Pie

Preheat oven to 350° Fahrenheit.

Ingredients:

prepared piecrust
½ cup melted butter
1 cup light corn syrup
2 tablespoons Kentucky bourbon
1 cup sugar
4 eggs
½ cup chocolate chips
1 cup pecans or walnuts

Cooking utensils you'll need:
measuring cups
measuring spoons
mixing bowl
rubber spatula

Directions:

Mix melted butter with corn syrup and bourbon. Stir in sugar and eggs. Mix well and pour into unbaked piecrust. Sprinkle chocolate chips evenly across the pie. Use the spatula to push the chocolate chips down a little. Sprinkle nuts evenly across the top, and bake for 45 minutes (until *set*).

Tip:

The alcohol in the bourbon evaporates as the pie bakes.

Appalachian Food History

Bourbon is whiskey that is made with at least 51 percent corn mash. Ninety-five percent of the bourbon produced annually in the United States comes from Kentucky, and cooking with this ingredient has become a tradition in the Bluegrass State. Some people credit Elija Craig, a Baptist minister who also founded Georgetown College, with having developed this unique beverage in the late 1700s. Other people say that while Reverend Craig did make whiskey, it was not bourbon. They think the legend was invented during the late 1800s to discourage people who supported the temperance movement. We do know that American colonists used rye to make whiskey in the 1700s. During that time, settlers were enticed to move to Kentucky where they could get 400 acres of free land simply by building a cabin and planting a corn crop. Some Kentucky farmers decided to utilize their surplus corn to make whiskey. Later, more defining features were added to the production of Kentucky bourbon. Today Bardstown, Kentucky, calls itself the Bourbon Capital of the World and holds an annual Kentucky Bourbon Festival.

Appalachian Food History

You might be surprised to learn that this popular snack is an ancient food. In fact, the oldest popcorn ever found was approximately 5,600 years old. And some of it could still pop! Popcorn probably originated in Mexico. The Aztec, Inca, and Mayan cultures all ate popcorn. The members of some cultures also wore popped corn necklaces. This popular food was grown in many parts of North America. Archeologists have discovered that it was cultivated in Ontario, Canada, prior to A.D. 1200. It was one of the foods introduced to European settlers by American Indians, and was served at the first Thanksgiving. Colonists sometimes used popcorn as a cereal, eating it with milk or cream.

Kentucky Praline Popcorn

Ingredients:

4 quarts popped popcorn
2 cups chopped pecans
¾ cup butter
¾ cup brown sugar, packed

Cooking utensils you'll need:
popcorn popper
measuring cups
large bowl
saucepan

Directions:

Mix popped corn and nuts in large bowl. Melt butter in saucepan, stir in sugar, and heat through. Pour the butter mixture over the popcorn mixture, stir well, and enjoy.

Tip:

If you don't have a popcorn popper, plain microwave popcorn works just as well. Follow the directions on the bag.

Further Reading

Burchill, James, Linda J. Crider, Peggy Kendrick, and Maricia Wright Bonner. *Ghosts and Haunts from the Appalachian Foothills: Stories and Legends.* Nashville, Tenn.: Rutledge Hill Press, 1993.

Dabney, Joseph. *Smokehouse Ham, Spoon Bread & Scuppernong Wine: The Folklore and Art of Southern Appalachian Cooking.* Nashville, Tenn.: Cumberland House, 1998.

Garland Page, Linda and Eliot Wiggington (editors). *The Foxfire Book of Appalachian Cookery.* New York: Gramercy, 2001.

Johnson-Coleman, Lorraine. *Larissa's Bread Book: Baking Bread and Telling Tales With Women of the American South.* Nashville, Tenn.: Rutledge Hill Press, 2001.

O'Brien, John. *At Home in the Heart of Appalachia.* New York: Alfred A. Knopf, 2001.

Rosenbaum, Stephanie. *Honey: From Flower to Table.* San Francisco, Calif.: Chronicle Books LLC, 2002.

The Art Institutes. *American Regional Cuisine: A Coast-to-Coast Celebration of the Nation's Culinary Diversity—With 250 Recipes.* New York: John Wiley & Sons, 2002.

Tice White, Betsy. *Mountain Folk, Mountain Food: Down-Home Wisdom, Plain Tales and Recipe Secrets from Appalachia.* Baltimore, Maryland: Recovery Communications, Inc. 1997.

Walker, Melissa. *All We Knew Was to Farm: Rural Women in the Upcountry South, 1919-1941.* Baltimore, Maryland: Johns Hopkins University Press, 2000.

For More Information

Appalachian Music
www.mustrad.org.uk/articles/appalach.htm

Catfish Recipes
www.catfishinstitute.com

Daniel Boone
www.Is.net/~newriver/nc/wnc4.htm

Davy Crockett
www.aboutfamouspeople.com/article1024.html

Geologic History of Appalachian Mountains
www.appalachiantales.com/geologic_history.htm

History of the Appalachian Trail
www.appalachiantrail.org/about/history/

Kitchen Safety
www.premiersystems.com/recipes/kitchen-safety/cooking-safety.html

North Carolina Barbecue History
www.ibiblio.org/lineback/lex.htm

State Agricultural Profiles
www.agclassroom.org

State History
www.theus50.com

Publisher's note:
The Web sites listed on this page were active at the time of publication. The publisher is not responsible for Web sites that have changed their addresses or discontinued operation since the date of publication. The publisher will review and update the Web sites upon each reprint.

Index

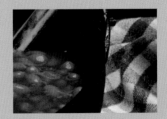

Picture Credits

PhotoDisc: cover, pp. 10, 16, 18, 27, 28, 31, 46, 48, 68; Photos.com: cover, pp. 9, 15, 18, 25, 37, 41, 42, 45, 56, 61, 69; Benjamin Stewart: pp. 15, 18, 21, 23, 32, 34, 38, 52, 54, 57, 58, 62, 63, 64, 69; Sharon Stewart: pp. 12, 19, 68, 72

Author:

In addition to writing, Joyce Libal has worked as an editor for a half dozen magazines, including a brief stint as recipe editor at *Vegetarian Gourmet*. Most of her experience as a cook, however, has been gained as the mother of three children and occasional surrogate mother to several children from different countries and cultures. She is an avid gardener and especially enjoys cooking with fresh herbs and vegetables and with the abundant fresh fruit that her husband grows in the family orchard.

Recipe Tester / Food Preparer:

Bonni Phelps owns How Sweet It Is Café in Vestal, New York. Her love of cooking and feeding large crowds comes from her grandmothers on both sides whom also took great pleasure in large family gatherings.

Consultant:

The Culinary Institute of America is considered the world's premier culinary college. It is a private, not-for-profit learning institution, dedicated to providing the world's best culinary education. Its campuses in New York and California provide learning environments that focus on excellence, leadership, professionalism, ethics, and respect for diversity. The institute embodies a passion for food with first-class cooking expertise.

Recipe Contributor:

Patricia Therrien has worked for several years with Harding House Publishing Service as a researcher and recipe consultant—but she has been experimenting with food and recipes for the past thirty years. Her expertise has enriched the lives of friends and family. Patty lives in western New York State with her family and numerous animals, including several horses, cats, and dogs.